WUNDERK

PIANO FOR PRESCHOOLERS

BOOK 3
2ND EDITION

An Introduction To WunderKeys

When I left home for college many years ago, I took with me a trunkful of clothes, a few pairs of shoes, a blanket, a pillow, and my favorite book, *Harold and the Purple Crayon*.

The book was torn, tattered, and loved to death.

As a young child, I needed my parents' help to cross the street or tie my shoes, but when I flipped through the pages of *Harold and the Purple Crayon*, I entered a world of inspiring adventures where I could do anything and be anyone.

So when I created WunderKeys with my husband, Trevor, we did so with one overriding goal in mind: to produce **piano method books** that would one day be packed into the trunk of a car – torn, tattered, and loved to death by a lifelong music student starting out on a new adventure.

Thank you for taking your piano students on our "wunderful" journey through music.

Andrea and Trevor Dow

Book 3

After completing *WunderKeys Piano For Preschoolers: Book 2*, preschoolers are ready to advance their exploration of the piano with their newly-acquired skills. *WunderKeys Piano For Preschoolers: Book 3* continues the learning in ways that are accessible and appropriate for this age group. All lessons are geared toward having young children understand everything they will need to know before learning to read notated music. Students will:

1. Play simple, pattern-based piano pieces on black keys
2. Read **off-staff rhythmic notation** (quarter, half, whole notes)
3. Recognize **directional movement in note reading**
4. Explore note stems pointing up and note stems pointing down
5. Listen for quarter, half, and whole notes
6. Learn **math skills** to assist musical understanding

Note: All instructions in this book are written from the perspective of a teacher speaking to a student and are intended to be read aloud.

A Rhythm Rhyme Welcome

After reading each stanza, I will say/clap the rhythm. Use your RH Pinky to play the rhythm back on a black key.

Pinky, won't you clean your room? Pointer Panda's coming soon!
It is hard to pick and choose. Play with me and pick up shoes!

Pink - y   Pig   clean your room!

Pinky, won't you clean your room? Middleton is coming soon!
Make it tidy; take a look. Play with me and pick up books!

Please pick   up   your   toys!

Pinky, won't you clean your room? Thumbelina's coming soon!
What should go inside this box? Play with me and pick up socks!

Pink - y   Pig   clean your room!

Pinky, won't you clean your room? Your friend Ringo's coming soon!
Make room for the girls and boys. Play with me and pick up toys!

Please pick   up   your   toys!

Pinky, won't you clean your room? All your friends will be here soon!
Look around, you messy guy. Your room's still a piggy sty!

The Hog Podge House

"I'm supposed to be cleaning up my room," whispered Pinky.
"I found this on the ground. What do you think it is?"

A

Pinky found this quarter note under his bed. It must have fallen out of his music book!

• • • • • • • • • • • • •

In music, we play a sound for one beat when we see a **quarter note**.

On a piece of paper, I will draw ten short, vertical lines. Can you draw solid ovals at the bottom of each line to make quarter notes?

B

On the piece of paper from Step A, tap each quarter note with your RH Pinky. Say, "Oink" each time you tap.

Try tapping again using your LH Middleton. Say, "Squeak" for each tap. Try tapping with any finger. Say, "One" each time you tap a quarter note.

C

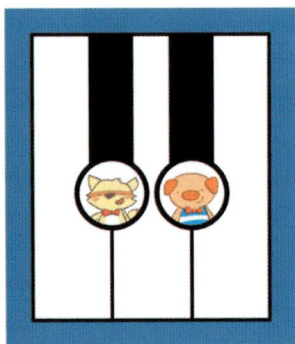

Place your RH Ringo and Pinky on a group of two black keys. Practice playing the pieces on the right.

Note: The dashed lines assist students in visualizing directional movement.

Listen as I call out a number. Play the piece that matches the number called.

1
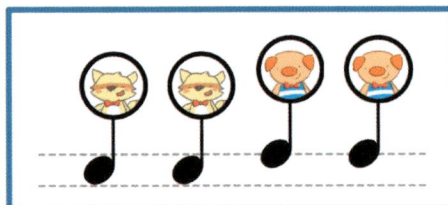

2
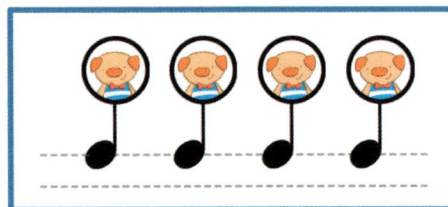

3
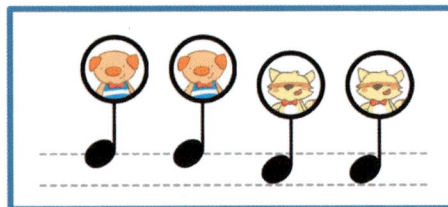

The Hog Podge House

1

We will play our parts separately. I will play lines 1, 3, and 5, and you will play lines 2 and 4.

2

Place your RH Ringo and Pinky on a group of two black keys.

Happily

mf

I know my room's mess - y, but it makes me so glad!
When my room is mess - y, I'm nev - er, ev - er sad!

with pedal

I could try to clean it up. I'd use a mop and broom.
But if it is squeak - y clean it's not a pigg - y room!

I know my room's mess - y, but mess - y's what I like!

The dashed lines in the student part assist with visualizing directional movement and do not represent a staff.

The Hog Podge House

1. Count the objects in Section 1. Place a check mark in the circle that holds the matching number.

2. In the *Ten Frame*, color a number of squares that matches the number of objects in Section 1.

3. Repeat Steps 1 and 2 for Section 2. Compare the colored squares in the two *Ten Frames*. Which section contains more objects?

4. Complete the pattern at the bottom of the page by drawing the correct object in the empty box.

1

7   2   3

2

5   4   1

3

Use this game with Lesson 1 and Lesson 2.

Players: 2 players   **Materials:** one game board, 18 coins, one die

Game Objectives:

Musical Objective: To count quarter notes
Game Objective: To remove coins from the game board

Setting It Up:

The student should sit on the floor with the game board placed in front, and the die and 18 coins placed to the side.

How To Play:

1. Before the game begins, the teacher places nine coins over any nine "junk" images on the game board.

2. The teacher taps a steady beat and then plays a set of quarter notes followed by a second set of quarter notes that contains more or fewer quarter notes than the first set.

3. The student determines if the **second set of quarter notes** played by the teacher contained more or fewer quarter notes than the first set, and then rolls the die.

4. If the second set of quarter notes played by the teacher in Step 2 contained more quarter notes than the first set, the student **adds a number of coins to the game board** (placing them over empty "junk" images) that corresponds with the number rolled in Step 3. If the second set of quarter notes played by the teacher in Step 2 contained fewer quarter notes than the first set, the student **removes a number of coins from the game board** that corresponds with the number rolled in Step 3.

5. Steps 2-4 are repeated until one of three things happens: 1. all coins have been removed from the junk images on the game board (the student wins), 2. all junk images on the game board have been covered with coins (the teacher wins), or 3. eight rounds have been played and the game is over. At this point the coins are counted. If more coins have been removed from the game board than are still remaining, the student wins. If more coins remain on the game board than have been removed, the teacher wins.

Note:

1. The student is not required to complete the game procedure independently. It is important that the teacher guides the student through the different steps of the game in a collaborative learning process.

A Rhythm Rhyme Welcome

After reading each stanza, I will say/clap the rhythm. Use your LH Pointer to play the rhythm back on a black key.

Hiking through the woods they go. Pinky stops and says, "Uh-oh!"
Find a rock or find a stump. Play with me to make him jump!

Don't   fall   in   the   brook!

Why did Ringo stop so fast? Oh! A brook! How will he pass?
Find a rock or find a stump. Play with me to make him jump!

Jump!   Jump!   Cross   the   ri - ver!

Middleton has dainty toes. "I can't get these wet, you know!"
Find a rock or find a stump. Play with me to make him jump!

Don't   fall   in   the   brook!

Pointer wants to take a nap. "I'll lay here and read our map."
Find a rock or find a stump. Play with me to make him jump!

Jump!   Jump!   Cross   the   ri - ver!

Thumbelina starts to grin, takes a breath, and jumps right in!
Give a cheer and shout, "Hooray!" Our friends got across today!

Brook Busters

"This is a tricky stream to cross," said Thumbelina,
"But don't worry, elephants always bring their swimming trunks!"

A

Hop To It!

I will place a long piece of tape on the floor. You will stand behind the taped line.

• • • • • • • • • • • • • • • • • • • •

Listen as I tap a steady beat while playing one, two, *or* three quarter notes on the piano.

Hop back and forth over the tape according to the number of quarter notes you hear. Let's play again!

B

Play quarter notes with your RH Pointer on any black key. Say, "Chomp" every time you play a quarter note.

Play quarter notes with your other Wunderbies. What one-beat words might they say as they play?

C

Place your RH Pointer, Middleton, and Ringo on a group of three black keys. Practice playing the pieces on the right.

Note: The dashed lines assist students in visualizing directional movement.

Listen as I call out a number. Play the piece that matches the number called.

1
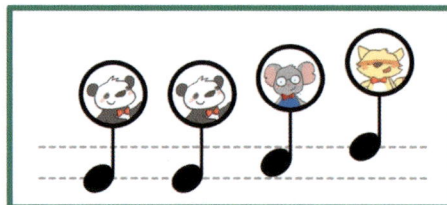

2
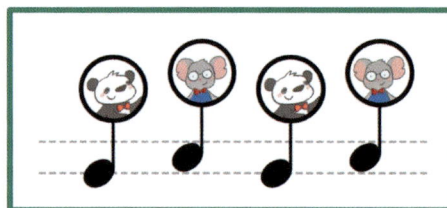

3

Brook Busters

1 We will play our parts separately. I will play lines 1, 3, and 5, and you will play lines 2 and 4.

2 Place your RH Pointer, Middleton, and Ringo on a group of three black keys.

Swing the eighths

mf Five friends were hik - ing in the woods, they came a-cross a stream!

with pedal

How will they find a way a - cross, with - out soak - ing their paws?

Thum - be - lin - a says "Jump in! The on - ly way is to swim!"

The dashed lines in the student part assist with visualizing directional movement and do not represent a staff.

Brook Busters

1. Count the leaves in Section 1. Place a check mark in the circle that holds the matching number.

2. In the *Ten Frame*, color a number of squares that matches the number of leaves in Section 1.

3. Repeat Steps 1 and 2 for Section 2. Compare the colored squares in the two *Ten Frames*. Which section contains more leaves?

4. Complete the pattern at the bottom of the page by drawing the correct animal in the empty box.

1

(5) (1) (9)

2

(7) (3) (2)

3

A Rhythm Rhyme Welcome

After reading each stanza, I will clap the rhythm. Use your RH Middleton to play the rhythm back on a black key.

Three friends fishing in the sun. Three friends having lots of fun.
Cast a line and make a wish. Play with me a tune for fish!

Let's   go   catch   a   fish!

Pinky tries to call them close. Pointer's dipping in his toes.
Cast a line and make a wish. Play with me a tune for fish!

Here   fish - y   fish!

Middleton tries switching bait. Quickly 'fore it gets too late!
Cast a line and make a wish. Play with me a tune for fish!

Let's   go   catch   a   fish!

Is that Ringo with a net? Dripping, smiling, soaking wet?
He caught one just as they wished! Play with me a tune for fish!

Here   fish - y   fish!

Four friends fishing in the sun, Ringo joins them in their fun.
If they use both rod and net, lots of fish is what they'll get!

3

"Heeeeere fishy, fishy, fishy!" sang Pinky.
"You can't call fish," Middleton giggled. "You have to catch them!"

A

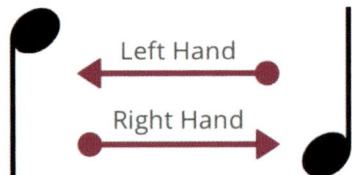

Left Hand

Right Hand

I will trace your hands on a piece of paper and then draw five stem-up and five stem-down quarter notes around the tracings. I will place a coin over each quarter note.

Can you slide the coins off of the quarter notes and onto the correct hand images?

B

Place your LH Middleton and Pointer and your RH Pointer and Middleton on groups of two black keys.

I will point to a note above. If the stem is pointing down, play a sound with your LH Middleton. If the stem is pointing up, play a sound with your RH Middleton.

C

Place your LH Ringo, Middleton, and Pointer and your RH Pointer, Middleton, and Ringo on groups of three black keys. Practice playing the pieces on the right.

Note: The dashed lines assist students in visualizing directional movement.

Listen as I call out a number. Play the piece that matches the number called.

1

2

3

1

We will play our parts separately. I will play lines 1, 3, and 5, and you will play lines 2 and 4.

2

Place your RH Pointer, Middleton, and Ringo and LH Ringo, Middleton, and Pointer on groups of three black keys.

Cheerfully

mf   Here fish-y fish-y,   to   catch you is our wish-y,   to   keep you as a   pet!

You're in the wa-ter,   the   sun is get-ting hot-ter,   and   we still have-n't   caught you yet!

Rin-go has a snor-kle,   he'll   jump in the wa-ter   and   chase you with a   net!

The dashed lines in the student part assist with visualizing directional movement and do not represent a staff.

Hooked On Fun

1. Count the fish in Section 1. Place a check mark in the circle that holds the matching number.

2. In the *Ten Frame*, color a number of squares that matches the number of fish in Section 1.

3. Repeat Steps 1 and 2 for Section 2. Compare the colored squares in the two *Ten Frames*. Which section contains more fish?

4. Complete the pattern at the bottom of the page by filling in the empty box with the correct color.

1

(1)   (6)   (5)

2

(4)   (9)   (3)

3

Hooked On Fun

Use this game with Lesson 3 and Lesson 4.

Players: 1 player   **Materials:** one game board, 10 coins

Game Objectives:

Musical Objective: To reinforce knowledge of LH and RH stem directions
Game Objective: To remove coins from the fish

Setting It Up:

The student should sit on the floor with the game board placed in front. One coin should be placed over each fish image on the game board, concealing the colored marks.

How To Play:

1. To begin the game, the teacher asks the student to choose one of the following colors: green or orange. The student's selection becomes the "target color."

2. Next, the teacher **points to the student's left hand or right hand.**

3. The student determines if the hand selected by the teacher in Step 2 is her right hand or left hand. If it is her right hand, the student removes one coin covering a fish that is located on the **stem-up side of the game board.** If it is her left hand, the student removes one coin covering a fish that is located on the **stem-down side of the game board.**

4. After removing the coin in Step 3, the student examines the colored dot on the fish revealed by the removed coin. If the colored dot **matches the "target color" selected in Step 1,** the student gives the coin to the teacher. If the colored dot does not match the "target color" selected in Step 1, the coin remains with the student.

5. Steps 2-4 are repeated **until the teacher collects three coins**. At this point the game is over. The teacher calculates the student's score by counting the number of coins in the student's possession. In future games, the student can attempt to beat this score.

Notes:

1. The educational value of this game is maximized when the teacher's choice in hands is unpredictable (i.e. don't simply alternate back and forth between left hand and right hand).

2. The student is not required to complete the game procedure independently. It is important that the teacher guides the student through the different steps of the game in a collaborative learning process.

A Rhythm Rhyme Welcome

After reading each stanza, I will say/clap the rhythm. Use your LH Pinky to play the rhythm back on a black key.

When it's muddy in his sty, Pinky Pig's a playful guy!
Muddy, dancing, happy pig. Play with me and splash so big!

Find   a   deep   mud - dy   pud - dle!

He likes mud between his toes. He likes mud upon his nose.
Muddy, dancing, happy pig. Play with me and splash so big!

Pink - y   in   the   mud!

Pinky dancing in the muck, don't go deep, please; don't get stuck!
Muddy, dancing, happy pig. Play with me and splash so big!

Find   a   deep   mud - dy   pud - dle!

Dirty ears and squishy feet, Pinky thinks that mud is neat.
Muddy, dancing, happy pig. Play with me and splash so big!

Pink - y   in   the   mud!

He is covered head to toe. Pinky, you are wet you know!
See that mud go squish and squash. Jump once more; now home to wash!

Mud Puddle Mambo

"Pinky! Where have you been all morning?" asked Pointer.
"Making mud pies," Pinky replied. "My sty was lovely and squishy today."

A

Why is Pinky Pig so happy? He found a half note to go with his quarter note!

. . . .

In music, we play a sound for two beats when we see a **half note**.

On a piece of paper, I will draw ten short, **vertical lines**. Can you draw "empty" ovals at the bottom of each of these lines to make half notes?

B

On the piece of paper from Step A, tap and hold each half note with your RH Pinky. Say, "Mud-dy" as you hold each tap.

Try it again with any finger. Say, "One-two" as you hold each tap.

C

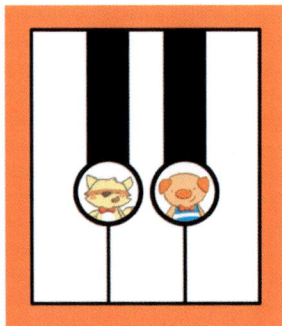

Place your RH Ringo and Pinky on a group of two black keys. Practice playing the pieces on the right.

Note: The dashed lines assist students in visualizing directional movement.

Listen as I call out a number. Play the piece that matches the number called.

1
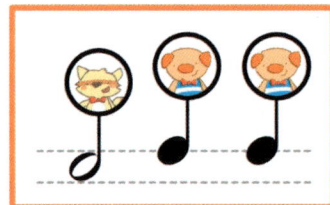

2
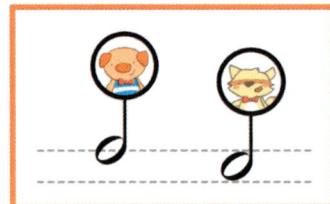

3

Mud Puddle Mambo

1 We will play our parts separately. I will play lines 1, 3, and 5, and you will play lines 2 and 4.

2 Place your RH Ringo and Pinky on a group of two black keys.

Excitedly

mf When I see mud - dy pud - dles, I jump right in!

Oh that mud makes me gig - gle and my legs start to wig - gle

Won't you join in? Come and dance with me! Mam - bo in mud!

The dashed lines in the student part assist with visualizing directional movement and do not represent a staff.

Mud Puddle Mambo

1. Count the puddles in Section 1. Place a check mark in the circle that holds the matching number.

2. In the *Ten Frame*, color a number of squares that matches the number of puddles in Section 1.

3. Repeat Steps 1 and 2 for Section 2. Compare the colored squares in the two *Ten Frames*. Which section contains more puddles?

4. Complete the pattern at the bottom of the page by drawing the correct letter in the empty box.

1

(4)   (5)   (6)

2

(3)   (5)   (1)

3

A   B   A   ☐   A   B

A Rhythm Rhyme Welcome

After reading each stanza, I will say/clap the rhythm. Use your RH Pointer to play the rhythm back on a black key.

Sitting in the meadow there, Pointer likes the warm fresh air.
What a sleepy little guy! Play with me a lullaby.

Sleep - y   pan - da   bear!

In the sun that he adores, Pointer Panda starts to snore.
What a sleepy little guy! Play with me a lullaby.

Lul - la - by,   close your eyes

Bugs and butterflies are there, but that panda doesn't care!
What a sleepy little guy! Play with me a lullaby.

Sleep - y   pan - da   bear!

Flutter 'round his fluffy head, snoozing on his grassy bed.
What a sleepy little guy! Play with me a lullaby.

Lul - la - by,   close your eyes

Now the sun has gone away. Pointer, don't you want to play?
Sleeping in the buttercups, clap one time to wake him up!

BEARied In Butterflies

"Butterflies are so peaceful," Pointer sighed.
"I'll just lay down here in the grass and take a little nap."

A

I will draw ten flowers on a piece of paper and give you ten coins.

Sit on the floor with the piece of paper and the coins. Listen as I tap a steady beat while playing four quarter notes or four half notes. If you hear half notes, cover two flowers with two coins. If you hear quarter notes, cover one flower with one coin.

Let's keep playing until a butterfly (coin) lands on every flower.

B

Place your RH Pointer, Middleton, and Ringo on a group of three black keys. I will do the same.

Listen and watch as I play a short melody that uses quarter notes and half notes. Can you copy the melody? Let's try again with a new melody.

C

Place your RH Pointer, Middleton, and Ringo on a group of three black keys. Practice playing the pieces on the right.

Note: The dashed lines assist students in visualizing directional movement.

Listen as I call out a number. Play the piece that matches the number called.

1

2

3

BEARied In Butterflies

Peacefully

1
We will play our parts separately. I will play lines 1, 3, and 5, and you will play lines 2 and 4.

2
Place your RH Pointer, Middleton, and Ringo on a group of three black keys.

mp But - ter - flies in the sky, pink and orange and blue!

Mak - ing me fall a - sleep and dream of bam - boo!

Watch them fly! Say "Good - night!"

with pedal

The dashed lines in the student part assist with visualizing directional movement and do not represent a staff.

BEARied In Butterflies

1. Count the flowers in Section 1. Place a check mark in the circle that holds the matching number.

2. In the *Ten Frame*, color a number of squares that matches the number of flowers in Section 1.

3. Repeat Steps 1 and 2 for Section 2. Compare the colored squares in the two *Ten Frames*. Which section contains more flowers?

4. Complete the pattern at the bottom of the page by drawing the correct flower in the empty box.

1

2   4   8

2

1   5   3

3

BEARiED in ButterFLiES

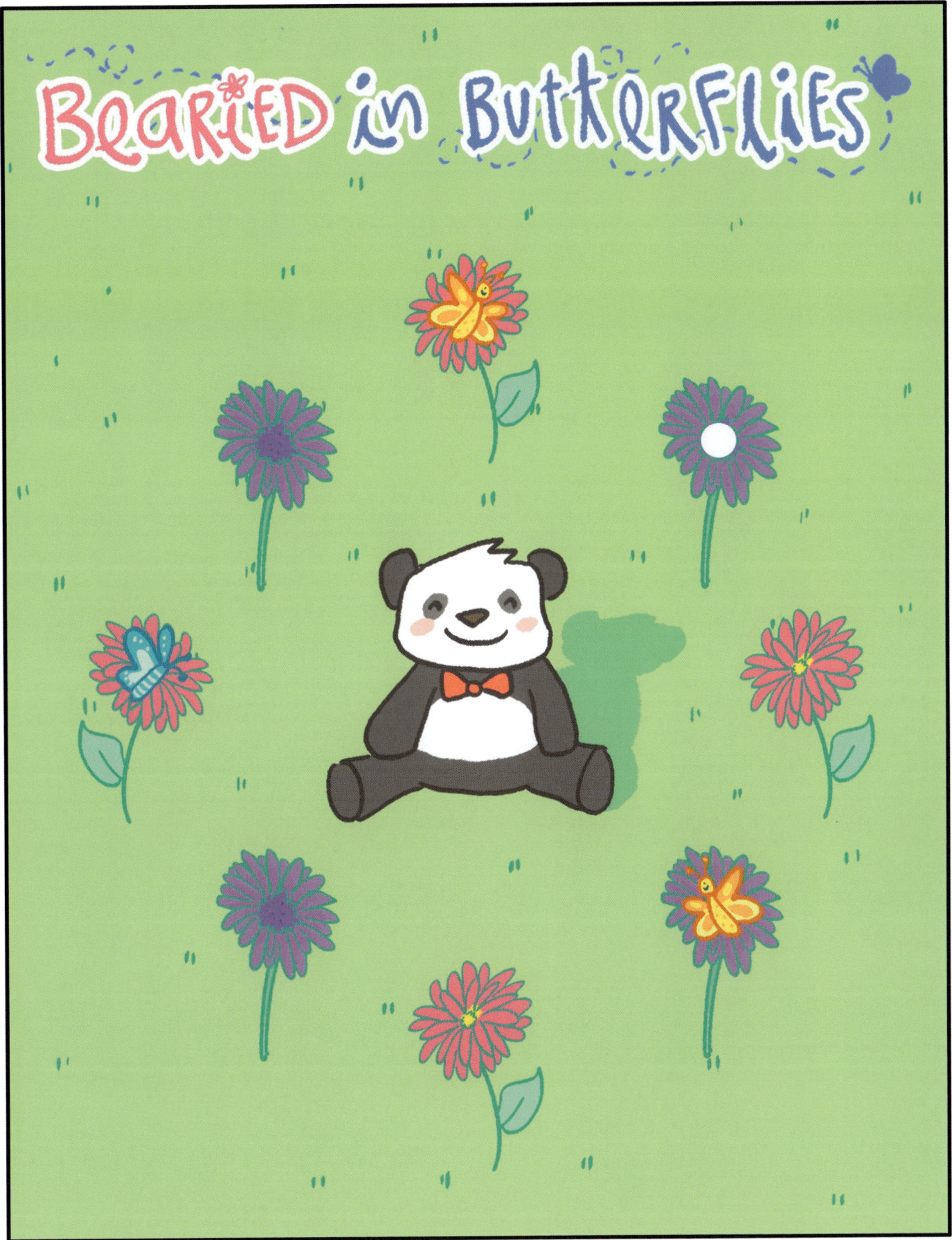

Use this game with Lesson 5 and Lesson 6.

Players: 1 player   **Materials:** one game board, 20 coins, one game marker, one cup

Game Objectives:

Musical Objective: To reinforce aural recognition of quarter notes and half notes
Game Objective: To collect coins (butterflies)

Setting It Up:

The student should sit on the floor with the game board placed in front, the cup placed over the image of Pointer, the game marker placed on the flower marked with the white circle, and the 20 coins placed to the side.

How To Play:

1 To begin, the teacher taps a steady beat while playing four quarter notes or four half notes.

2 The student determines if the sounds played by the teacher were quarter notes or half notes, and then moves the game marker clockwise around the circle of flowers: **one space** if quarter notes were played or **two spaces** if half notes were played.

3 After moving the game marker, the student analyzes the flower game square where the game marker is resting. If the game marker is on a flower with a butterfly, the student collects one coin from beside the game board and places it in the cup. If the game marker is on an empty flower, the first round is over.

4 Steps 1-3 are **repeated 10 more times.** At this point, the student and teacher count the number of coins in the cup to determine the student's score. In future games the student attempts to beat this score.

Note:

1 The student is not required to complete the game procedure independently. It is important that the teacher guides the student through the different steps of the game in a collaborative learning process.

A Rhythm Rhyme Welcome

After reading each stanza, I will say/clap the rhythm. Use your LH Ringo to play the rhythm back on a black key.

Pinky's calling from the trees, "Ringo come and play with me!"
Climb the ladder to the top. Play with me so he won't stop!

Up   in   the   tree house!

Ringo loves to climb up high. He is quick, and he is spry!
Climb the ladder to the top. Play with me so he won't stop!

Lad - der   to   the   leaves!

Here's a ladder to the leaves, where the friends hide in the trees.
Climb the ladder to the top. Play with me so he won't stop!

Up   in   the   tree house!

Ringo's almost reached the fort. Pinky gives a happy snort!
Climb the ladder to the top. Play with me so he won't stop!

Lad - der   to   the   leaves!

Pinky, Ringo in the tree, is there room up there for me?
Climb the ladder; that's the way. Up the steps and now we play!

Ladder To The Leaves

"Ringo! Come and play in my tree house!" called Pinky.
"Oh boy!" said Ringo. "Raccoons love being up in the leaves!"

A

I will trace your hands on a piece of paper and then draw a variety of stem-up and stem-down quarter and half notes around the tracings. I will place a coin over each note.

Sit beside the piece of paper and listen to my instructions.

If I say, "Two beats," slide a coin off of any half note and onto the correct hand image. If I say, "One beat," slide a coin off of any quarter note and onto the correct hand image.

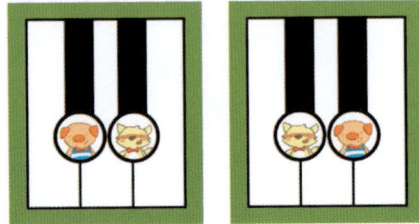

B

Place your LH Pinky and Ringo and your RH Ringo and Pinky on groups of two black keys.

Listen as I clap a quarter note/half note rhythm. Play back the rhythm with your LH Pinky. Play back the rhythm with your RH Ringo.

C

Place your LH Pinky and Ringo and your RH Ringo and Pinky on groups of two black keys.

Note: The dashed lines assist students in visualizing directional movement.

Listen as I call out a number. Play the piece that matches the number called.

1

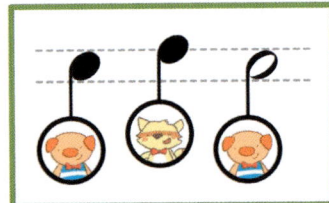

2

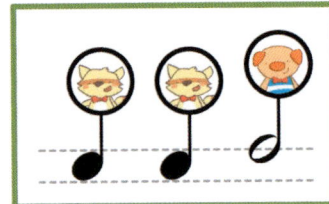

3

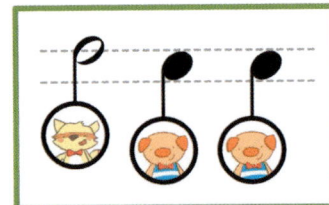

Ladder To The Leaves

1

We will play our parts separately. I will play lines 1, 3, and 5, and you will play lines 2 and 4.

2

Place your LH Pinky and Ringo and your RH Ringo and Pinky on groups of two black keys.

Sweetly

mf Rin - go, climb my | lad - der to the leaves! | Rin - go, won't you | come and play with me?

with pedal

Climb up to my tree house, | we'll have so much fun! | There is lots of room for | ev - 'ry - one!

Rin - go, climb my | lad - der to the leaves! | Where it's great to | play a - mong the trees!

The dashed lines in the student part assist with visualizing directional movement and do not represent a staff.

Ladder To The Leaves

1. Count the houses in Section 1. Place a check mark in the circle that holds the matching number.

2. In the *Ten Frame*, color a number of squares that matches the number of houses in Section 1.

3. Repeat Steps 1 and 2 for Section 2. Compare the colored squares in the two *Ten Frames*. Which section contains more houses?

4. Complete the pattern at the bottom of the page by drawing the correct object in the empty box.

1

(5) (2) (3)

2

(7) (3) (2)

3

A Rhythm Rhyme Welcome

After reading each stanza, I will say/clap the rhythm. Use your RH Thumbelina to echo the rhythm on a black key.

Thumbelina likes to stroll to her favorite water hole.
Baboons doing belly flops... Play with me and watch them drop!

Ba - boons   do - ing   bel - ly   flops!

When the sun begins to set, Thumbelina gets all wet!
Baboons doing belly flops... Play with me and watch them drop!

Splash - ing   in   the   wa - ter!

Swimming with her monkey buds, playing in the slipp'ry mud.
Baboons doing belly flops... Play with me and watch them drop!

Ba - boons   do - ing   bel - ly   flops!

Look at all the splashing fun, while they watch the setting sun.
Baboons doing belly flops... Play with me and watch them drop!

Splash - ing   in   the   wa - ter!

When the stars begin to shine, Thumbelina says, "It's time."
Dripping wet and full of glee, baboons climb back up the tree!

Belly Floppin' with Baboons

"Oh! It's going to be a beautiful sunset tonight!" exclaimed Thumbelina.
"I think I'll watch the sun go down from my favorite watering hole!"

A

I will draw three whole notes on a piece of paper. Can you draw three more whole notes on the same piece of paper?

Tap and hold each whole note with your RH Thumbelina. Each time you tap and hold say, "Thum-be-lin-a."

B

In music, we play a sound for four beats when we see a whole note.

On the piece of paper from Step A, tap and hold each whole note with any finger. Say, "One-two-three-four" for each tap and hold.

C

Place your RH Thumbelina and Pointer on a group of two black keys. Practice playing the pieces on the right.

Note: The dashed lines assist students in visualizing directional movement.

Listen as I call out a number. Play the piece that matches the number called.

1
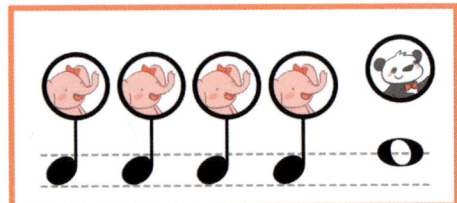

2
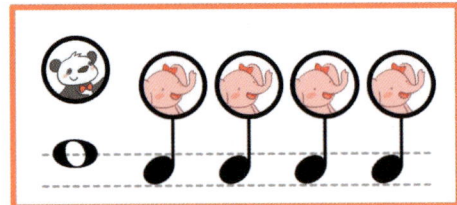

3
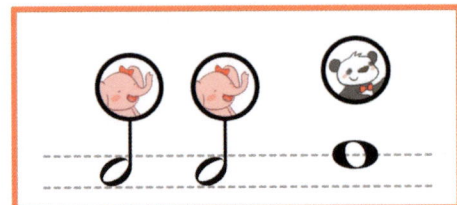

Belly Floppin' with Baboons

1 We will play our parts separately. I will play lines 1, 3, and 5, and you will play lines 2 and 4.

2 Place your RH Thumbelina and Pointer on a group of two black keys.

Playfully

mf Bel - ly flop-pin', | there's no stop-pin' | those ba-boons when | Thum-be-lin-a's near!

In the wa-ter, | tee-ter tott-ter. | In the branch es | they all cheer!

Bel - ly flop-pin', | there's no stop-pin'... | ba- | boons!

The dashed lines in the student part assist with visualizing directional movement and do not represent a staff.

Belly Floppin' with Baboons

1. Count the baboons in Section 1. Place a check mark in the circle that holds the matching number.

2. In the *Ten Frame*, color a number of squares that matches the number of baboons in Section 1.

3. Repeat Steps 1 and 2 for Section 2. Compare the colored squares in the two *Ten Frames*. Which section contains more baboons?

4. Complete the pattern at the bottom of the page by drawing the correct letter in the empty box.

1

(8)   (2)   (4)

2

(2)   (1)   (9)

3

A   A   B   ☐   A   A   B   B

Belly Floppin' with Baboons

Use this game with Lesson 7 and Lesson 8.

Players: 2 players   **Materials:** one game board, 20 coins, one die

Game Objectives:

Musical Objective: To reinforce aural recognition of half notes and whole notes
Game Objective: To collect coins from the baboons on the game board

Setting It Up:

The student should sit on the floor with the game board placed in front and the 20 coins and the die placed to the side.

How To Play:

1 To begin, the student rolls the die and then uses coins to cover a number of baboon note images on the game board that corresponds with the number rolled. *For example, if the student rolls a "3," three coins are used to cover three baboon note images.*

2 Next, the teacher taps a steady beat while **playing two half notes or two whole notes.**

3 The student determines if the teacher played half notes or whole notes and then slides each of the coins placed in Step 1 to the side to examine the baboon note images underneath.

4 If a coin is resting on a baboon with a note image that **matches the note values** played by the teacher in Step 2, the coin is removed from the baboon and placed in the pond with Thumbelina. If a coin is resting on a baboon with a note image that **does not match** the notes played by the teacher in Step 2, the coin is removed and given to the teacher. *For example, if the teacher played two half notes, a coin resting on a baboon with a half note image is placed in the pond and a coin resting on a baboon with a whole note image is given to the teacher.*

5 After the coins from Round 1 have been moved to their correct locations (moved to the pond or given to the teacher) Steps 1-4 are repeated. Play continues **until a player collects 10 or more coins** and wins the game. Note: the coins placed in the pond belong to the student.

Note:

1 The student is not required to complete the game procedure independently. It is important that the teacher guides the student through the different steps of the game in a collaborative learning process.

A Rhythm Rhyme Welcome

After reading each stanza, I will clap the rhythm. Use your LH Middleton to play the rhythm back on a black key.

Big dogs, small dogs like to bark, playing in the big dog park.
Here's a brown dog running fast. Play with me as he goes past!

Bark! Bark! Woof!

Big dogs, small dogs like to bark, playing in the big dog park.
Here's a white dog with a stick. Play with me as she runs quick.

Mid - dle - ton,   walk - ing   dogs!

Big dogs, small dogs like to bark, playing in the big dog park.
Here's one with a spotted eye. Play with me as he runs by.

Bark! Bark! Woof!

Big dogs, small dogs like to bark, playing in the big dog park.
Here's one that is big and slow. Play with me and watch him go.

Mid - dle - ton,   walk - ing dogs!

Big dogs, small dogs like to bark, playing in the big dog park.
Here's a dog with hair that's flat. Meows at me... Whoops! That's a cat!

Dog Park Delight

"Whew! Keeping up with these dogs is hard work!" Middleton laughed. "This is a job for Ringo. He's much faster than me!"

A

I will give you a cup, twenty coins, and two dice. Listen as I tap a steady beat while playing a quarter, a half, or a whole note. Can you place a number of coins into the cup that corresponds with the number of beats received by the note value I played? Let's try it again four more times.

Next, **roll the dice** and then count the number of coins in the cup. If the number displayed on the dice is less than the number of coins in the cup, you win!

B

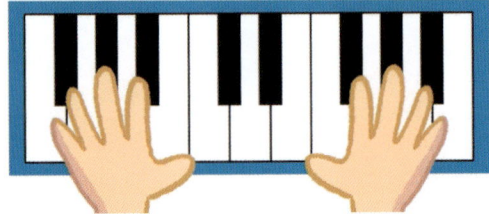

Place your hands on black keys as shown. I will tap a steady beat.

Play a quarter note **with each finger,** beginning with your LH Ringo. Play a half note with each finger. Play a whole note with each finger.

C

Place your RH Pointer, Middleton, and Ringo on a group of three black keys. Practice playing the pieces on the right.

Note: The dashed lines assist students in visualizing directional movement.

Listen as I call out a number. Play the piece that matches the number called.

1.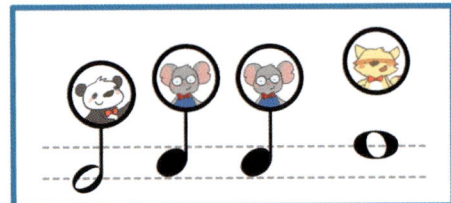

2.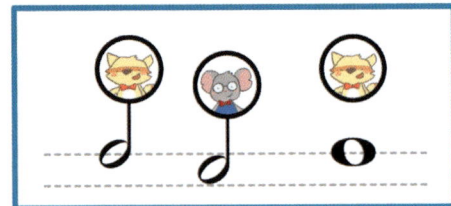

3.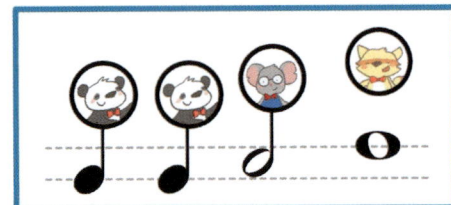

Dog Park Delight

1 We will play our parts separately. I will play lines 1, 3, and 5, and you will play lines 2 and 4.

2 Place your RH Pointer, Middleton, and Ringo on a group of three black keys.

With energy

mf Go - ing to the dog park! | Woof! Woof! Woof! | Where there's lots of fur - ry fun!

with pedal

Lit - tle dogs and pup - pies | Woof! Woof! Woof! | Run - ning af - ter ev - 'ry - one!

"Here boy!" | Woof! Woof! Woof! | "Now it's time to take a bath!" Woof!

The dashed lines in the student part assist with visualizing directional movement and do not represent a staff.

Dog Park Delight

1. Count the pets in Section 1. Place a check mark in the circle that holds the matching number.

2. In the *Ten Frame*, color a number of squares that matches the number of pets in Section 1.

3. Repeat Steps 1 and 2 for Section 2. Compare the colored squares in the two *Ten Frames*. Which section contains more pets?

4. Complete the pattern at the bottom of the page by drawing the correct pet in the empty box.

1

2   **4**   **8**

2

5   **6**   **1**

3

A Rhythm Rhyme Welcome

After reading each stanza, I will clap the rhythm. Use your RH Pointer to play the rhythm back on a black key.

Listen to the cows say, "Moo!" as they're munching on bamboo.
Lift those heavy bales of straw. Play with me and say, "Yeehaw!"

Play - ing   on   the   farm!

Listen to the rooster crow. Look at all the lettuce grow.
Listen to the chickens caw. Play with me and say, "Yeehaw!"

Yee - haw!   Poin - ter   Pan - da!

Pet the wooly heads of sheep. Hear the baby chicks go, "Peep!"
Watch out for the barn cat claws! Play with me and say, "Yeehaw!"

Play - ing   on   the   farm!

See the goats with curly horns, walking through the rows of corn.
Take a porch swing with Grandpa. Play with me and say, "Yeehaw!"

Yee - haw!   Poin - ter   Pan - da!

Pointer Panda's having fun on his tractor in the sun.
He's a farmer; it is true! Growing all his own bamboo!

Sleeping Panda Ranch

"Welcome to Sleeping Panda Ranch!" called Pointer. "We specialize in fresh eggs, fresh tomatoes, and fresh bamboo!"

A

I will give you a die and then draw a large quarter note, a large half note, and a large whole note on a piece of paper.

To begin, roll the die. If the number displayed on the die matches the beats received by one of the three note values on the piece of paper, cover the correct one with your hand.

Be quick... I will be racing to do the same! If the die displays a three, five, or six, roll again.

Let's play five times!

B

Place your hands as shown. I will point to a note value below. Play it using any finger on the correct hand.

C

Place your LH Ringo, Middleton, and Pointer and your RH Pointer, Middleton, and Ringo on groups of three black keys. Practice playing the pieces on the right.

Note: The dashed lines assist students in visualizing directional movement.

Listen as I call out a number. Play the piece that matches the number called.

1

2
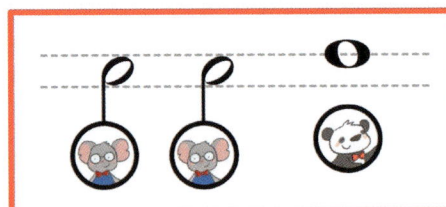

3

Sleeping Panda Ranch

1 We will play our parts separately. I will play lines 1, 3, and 5, and you will play lines 2 and 4.

2 Place your RH Pointer, Middleton, and Ringo and LH Ringo, Middleton, and Pointer on groups of three black keys.

Swing the eighths

mf Wel-come to Point- er's farm | ev -'ry day is sun - ny! | Wel-come to Point- er's farm | where the grass is green.

Lis - ten to the cows say, "Moo!" | on this farm that grows bam - boo!

When you're here play- ing in the | sun, | you will have lots of pan-da | fun!

The dashed lines in the student part assist with visualizing directional movement and do not represent a staff.

Sleeping Panda Ranch

1. Count the animals in Section 1. Place a check mark in the circle that holds the matching number.

2. In the *Ten Frame*, color a number of squares that matches the number of animals in Section 1.

3. Repeat Steps 1 and 2 for Section 2. Compare the colored squares in the two *Ten Frames*. Which section contains more animals?

4. Complete the pattern at the bottom of the page by drawing the correct animal in the empty box.

1

(4)   (6)   (5)

2

(8)   (2)   (7)

3

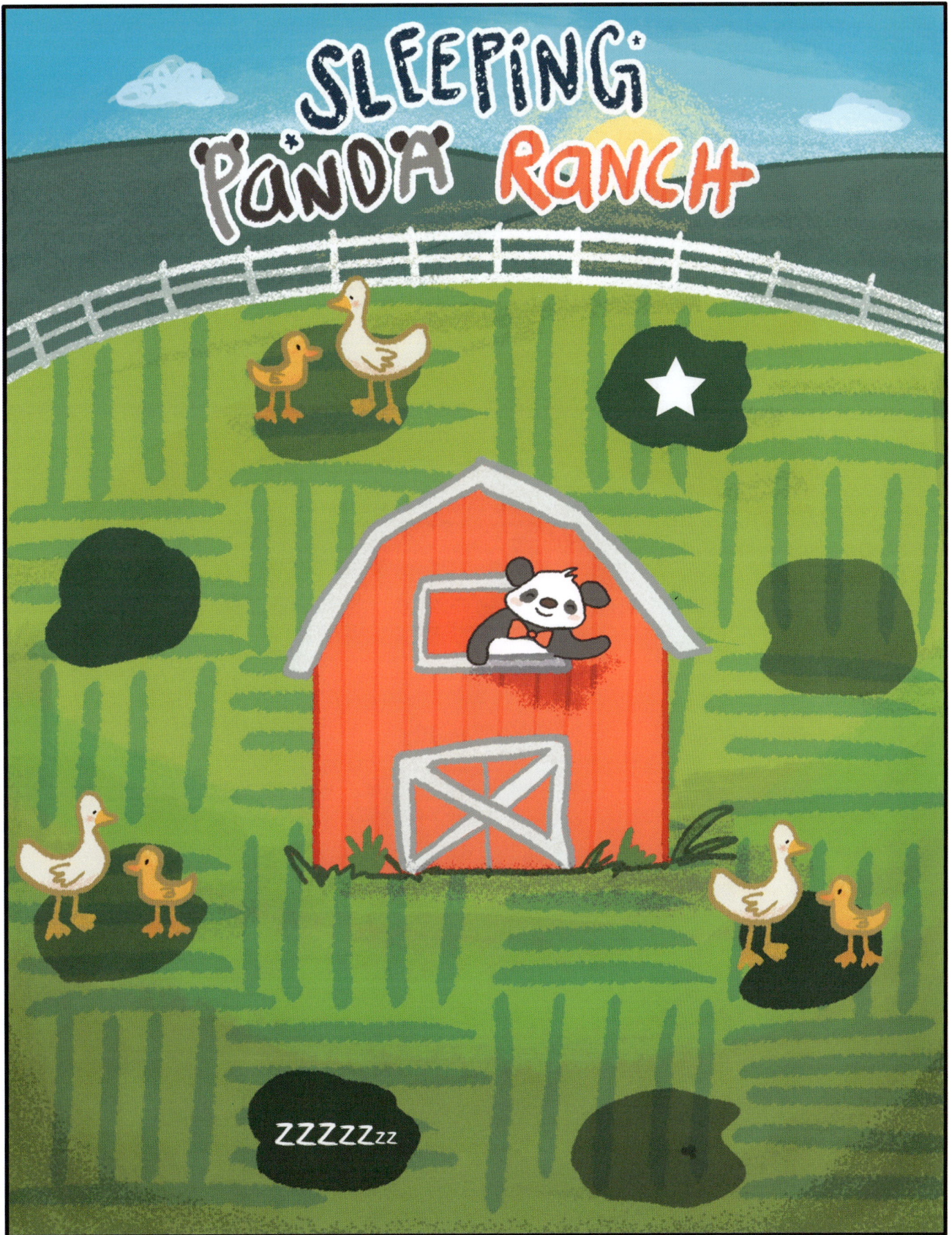

Use this game with Lesson 9 and Lesson 10.

Players: 1 player   **Materials:**   one game board, 10 coins, one game marker, one cup

Game Objectives:

Musical Objective: To reinforce aural recognition of quarter, half, and whole notes
Game Objective: To collect coins (duck eggs)

Setting It Up:

The student should sit on the floor with the game board placed in front, the 10 coins placed over the barn, the game marker placed on the dark green square marked with a star, and the cup placed to the side.

How To Play:

1 To begin, the teacher taps a steady beat while playing two quarter notes **or** two half notes **or** two whole notes.

2 The student determines if the sounds played by the teacher were quarter, half, or whole notes, and then moves the game marker clockwise around the circle of dark green squares: **one space** if quarter notes were played, **two spaces** if half notes were played, and **four spaces** if whole notes were played.

3 After moving the game marker, the student analyzes the dark green square where the game marker is resting. If the game marker is on an animal square, the student **collects one coin** from the barn and places it in the cup. If the game marker is on a blank square, the first round is over; and if it is on the square with the sleepy ZZZZZZZs, the game ends.

4 Assuming the game is not over, Steps 1-3 are repeated until the student's game marker **lands on the sleepy ZZZZZZZs,** ending the game. At this point, the student and teacher count the number of coins in the cup to determine the student's score. In future games the student attempts to beat this score.

Note:

1 The student is not required to complete the game procedure independently. It is important that the teacher guides the student through the different steps of the game in a collaborative learning process.

A Rhythm Rhyme Welcome

After reading each stanza, I will clap the rhythm. Use your LH Ringo to play the rhythm back on a black key.

Look at all that you can do, all the lessons you've worked through!
Graduation day's today; play with me to say, "Hooray!"

Grad - u - a - tion   day   to - day!

Quarter notes and half notes, too: you can play these; it is true!
Graduation day's today; play with me to say, "Hooray!"

Hoo - ray!   Play   it   loud!

Whole notes holding for four beats, lots of games and music treats!
Graduation day's today; play with me to say, "Hooray!"

Grad - u - a - tion   day   to - day!

Counting objects, I'm impressed! Knowing which has more or less.
Graduation day's today; play with me to say, "Hooray!"

Hoo - ray!   Play   it   loud!

You should be so very proud; stand up here and take a bow!
Shake my hand now, won't you, please? You're a star of WunderKeys!

The Muddy Tree Mystery

1. I am going to read the story and play the musical excerpts.

2. Then, I will read the story again while you play the musical excerpts.

3. Finally, we will invite your parents into the studio to experience our musical story.

I hear hammering. Does anyone else hear hammering?

It's coming from that tree up there.

BOOM! SMASH! BANG!

Pointer and Middleton can hear a hammering sound coming from the trees! Place your RH Pointer and Middleton on a group of two black keys and play the hammering tune below.

Eww! Why is mud dripping from the trees?

Hmmm... Hammering and mud? It's a mystery that I'm going to solve!

Ringo wants to climb the tree to solve the mystery. Place your LH Pinky and Ringo on a group of two black keys to play the climbing melody.

Climb,   Ring   -   o!   Climb,   Ring   -   o!

Any yummy leaves up there, Ringo?

Wow! Everyone, you have to come and see this!

Graduation Day

But what about Thumbelina? She can't climb trees.

That's what you think, Middleton! Watch this!

The Wunderbies want to cheer for Thumbelina! Place your RH Pointer, Middleton, and Ringo on a group of three black keys to play a cheer.

Thumb - be - li - na,   climb   to   the   top!

Oh! You all surprised me. How did you know I was here?

Mud doesn't usually fall from trees. It had to be you, Pinky.

The Wunderbies are excited about their new tree house! Place your LH Ringo, Middleton, and Pointer on a group of three black keys to play a happy tune.

In   our   new   tree   house   we'll   have   fun!

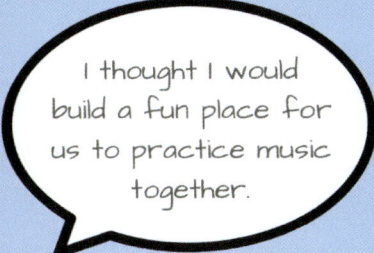

Graduation Day

1. Count the hats in Section 1. Place a check mark in the circle that holds the matching number.

2. In the *Ten Frame*, color a number of squares that matches the number of hats in Section 1.

3. Repeat Steps 1 and 2 for Section 2. Compare the colored squares in the two *Ten Frames*. Which section contains more hats?

4. Complete the pattern at the bottom of the page by filling in the empty box with the correct color.

1

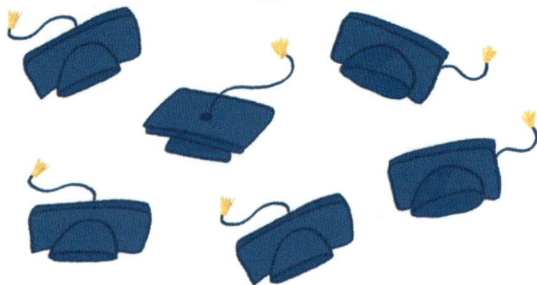

9   2   6

2

3   5   2

3

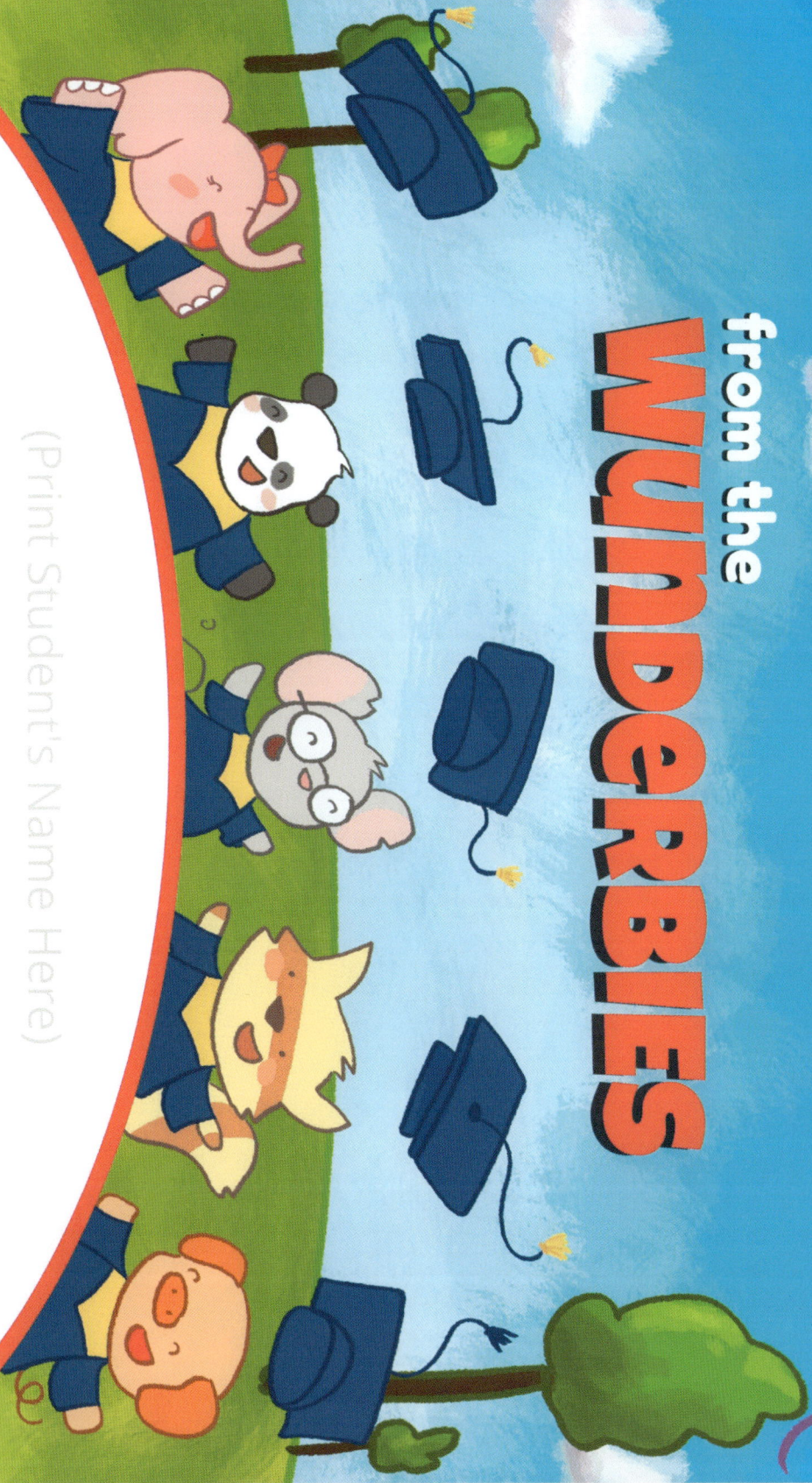

Certificate of Completion

CONGRATULATIONS
from the
WUNDERBIES

(Print Student's Name Here)

has completed WunderKeys Piano For Preschoolers - Book 3

Printed in Great Britain
by Amazon

27293438R00034